NVIDIA

REVOLUTION

*Driving AI, Gaming, and Computing Forward: A History,
Legacy of Innovation, Chip Evolution, and Industry
Challenges*

David E. Truitt

COPYRIGHT

TABLE OF CONTENTS

INTRODUCTION 1

    Overview of NVIDIA Corporation 1

CHAPTER 1 7

OPERATIONAL CHARACTERISTICS AND KEY PRODUCTS
....7

    GPU vs. CPU Technology 7

    CPUs: The Versatile Taskmasters 7

    GPUs: Masters of Parallel Processing 8

    Parallel Processing Capabilities of GPUs 9

    Advancements in Semiconductor Chip Capacity 11

    Key Products and Applications 12

CHAPTER 2 17

EARLY HISTORY (1990S) 17

    Founding of NVIDIA in 1993 17

    Key Breakthroughs in the 1990s 19

    Challenges and Triumphs 21

CHAPTER 3 23

GAMING EXPANSION AND DIVERSIFICATION (2000s) 23

    Role in Gaming Console Development 23

    Diversification into Real-World Applications 25

    Recognition and Setbacks 26

CHAPTER 4 28

THE RISE OF PARALLEL COMPUTING AND AI (2010s) 28

    Development of Parallel Computing 28

Introduction of CUDA in 2006...29

Impact on AI and Deep Learning Applications 30

Strategic Acquisitions 31

Mobile Computing and Automotive Innovations 32

The Broader Implications of Parallel Computing and AI 33

CHAPTER 5 35

THE AI RENAISSANCE AND MODERN CHALLENGES
(2020s) 35

AI Breakthroughs and GPU Advancements 35

Omniverse Platform for 3D Imaging and Design................36

Impact of ChatGPT and AI-Driven Demand for NVIDIA Chips
....37

Regulatory Scrutiny and Antitrust Challenges 38

Attempted Arm Ltd. Acquisition 39

Ongoing Investigations in the U.S., Europe, and China 40

CHAPTER 6 42

BLACKWELL INNOVATIONS AND THE FUTURE 42

Overview of Blackwell Architecture 42

Key Features 43

GB200 Grace Blackwell Superchip and Its Applications 44

AI-Focused Product and Software Advancements 44

DGX Cloud Platform and Partnerships with Cloud Service
Providers 45

Collaborations with Software Makers..................................46

CHAPTER 7 49

THE NVIDIA GEFORCE RTX 50-SERIES 49

Features of the RTX 50-Series...49

Blackwell Architecture Upgrades 50

Detailed Specifications 51

Comparison with Previous Generations 54

Advancements in Performance, Memory, and Energy Efficiency
....55

CHAPTER 8 58

NVIDIA'S IMPACT ON EMERGING TECHNOLOGIES.........58

Pioneering Artificial Intelligence (AI)..58

Enabling the Metaverse..59

Transforming Generative AI Models 61

Contributions to Key Industries...62

Future Directions for NVIDIA Technology....................................63

CONCLUSION...66

INTRODUCTION

Overview of NVIDIA Corporation

NVIDIA Corporation is a towering figure in technology, widely recognised as a global leader in graphics processing units (GPUs) and artificial intelligence (AI). Since its inception, NVIDIA has revolutionised the gaming industry and become a key driver of advancements in computing, AI, data science, and machine learning. Its innovative spirit and relentless pursuit of excellence have cemented its reputation as one of the most influential companies in the tech industry.

Founded in 1993 by Jensen Huang, Chris Malachowsky, and Curtis Priem, NVIDIA emerged during a rapid transformation in computing. The founders envisioned a company that would push the boundaries of technology and create solutions capable of addressing the complex challenges of digital computation. Today, NVIDIA's reach extends beyond its initial focus on gaming GPUs, influencing sectors such as healthcare, automotive, robotics, and cloud computing.

At the core of NVIDIA's success lies its unwavering commitment to innovation. The company's products and technologies have continually set new benchmarks, redefining the possibilities of what GPUs and AI can achieve. This commitment is reflected in its mission to solve the world's most pressing computational problems through a combination of cutting-edge technology and visionary leadership.

NVIDIA's journey to becoming a leader in GPU manufacturing began with the introduction of the GeForce 256 in 1999, which was heralded as the world's first GPU. This groundbreaking invention transformed the gaming industry by enabling real-time 3D graphics, a previously unimaginable feat. The GeForce 256's success set the stage for NVIDIA's dominance in the gaming market and highlighted the potential of GPUs to accelerate computational tasks across various domains.

Over the years, NVIDIA continued to innovate, releasing successive generations of GPUs that pushed the limits of performance and efficiency. The company's product portfolio expanded to include consumer and professional graphics cards catering to gamers, content creators, and scientists alike. NVIDIA's GPUs became synonymous with quality and performance, establishing the company as the go-to brand for anyone seeking cutting-edge graphics technology.

Beyond gaming, NVIDIA recognised the potential of GPUs to address broader computational challenges. This realisation led to the development of CUDA (Compute Unified Device Architecture) in 2006, a parallel computing platform and programming model that revolutionised how GPUs could be used for general-purpose computing. CUDA empowered researchers and developers to harness the immense computational power of GPUs for tasks such as scientific simulations, data analysis, and AI training, solidifying NVIDIA's position as a pioneer in the tech industry.

One of NVIDIA's most significant milestones came in 2022 with the breakthrough of OpenAI's ChatGPT, an advanced language model that captivated the world with its ability to generate human-like text. ChatGPT's success underscored the critical role that NVIDIA's GPUs played in enabling the development of such sophisticated AI models. The computational demands of training large language models like ChatGPT required immense processing power, which NVIDIA's GPUs were uniquely equipped to provide.

The NVIDIA A100 Tensor Core GPU, in particular, emerged as a game-changer in the AI landscape. Designed for high-performance computing and deep learning, the A100 became the backbone of AI training and inference workloads, powering advancements in natural language processing, computer vision, and other AI applications. By providing the hardware necessary to train models like ChatGPT, NVIDIA contributed to OpenAI's success and demonstrated its technology's transformative potential.

This partnership highlighted the symbiotic relationship between AI and GPU technology. As AI models grew more complex, the demand for robust and efficient GPUs increased, creating a virtuous cycle of innovation. NVIDIA's role in enabling breakthroughs like ChatGPT cemented its reputation as a key enabler of the AI revolution and reinforced its position as a leader in the tech industry.

NVIDIA's market dominance can be attributed to its relentless focus on innovation and ability to anticipate and adapt to emerging trends. The company's investments in research and development have consistently yielded groundbreaking technologies that set it apart from competitors. NVIDIA has consistently pushed the envelope of what's possible, from introducing real-time ray tracing with its RTX GPUs to developing specialised AI chips like the A100 and H100.

In addition to hardware, NVIDIA's software ecosystem has played a crucial role in its success. Platforms like NVIDIA Omniverse, a collaborative environment for 3D simulation and design, and NVIDIA DGX systems, purpose-built for AI research, exemplify the company's holistic approach to innovation. By providing integrated solutions that combine hardware and software, NVIDIA has created a seamless experience for developers and researchers, further solidifying its leadership in the tech industry.

NVIDIA's impact extends beyond technology to influence entire industries. In healthcare, for example, its GPUs accelerate medical imaging, drug discovery, and genomics research. In automotive, NVIDIA's DRIVE platform powers autonomous vehicles, enabling safer and more efficient transportation. In robotics, NVIDIA's technologies create intelligent machines capable of performing complex tasks. These applications highlight the versatility and transformative potential of NVIDIA's innovations.

The company's commitment to sustainability and social responsibility has also contributed to its market dominance. NVIDIA has prioritised energy efficiency in its product designs, recognising the importance of reducing the environmental impact of high-performance computing. By addressing the growing demand for sustainable technology solutions, NVIDIA has positioned itself as a responsible and forward-thinking leader in the tech industry.

Looking ahead, NVIDIA's role in shaping the future of technology remains undeniable. As AI continues to evolve and the demand for high-performance computing grows, NVIDIA's innovations will undoubtedly play a central role in driving progress. The company's legacy of excellence and its vision for the future ensure that it will remain at the forefront of technological advancement for years.

CHAPTER 1

OPERATIONAL CHARACTERISTICS AND KEY PRODUCTS

GPU vs. CPU Technology

The evolution of computational technology has consistently revolved around optimising performance, efficiency, and adaptability. The distinction between Graphics Processing Units (GPUs) and Central Processing Units (CPUs) is at the heart of this pursuit. Understanding their fundamental differences is key to appreciating their individual and combined contributions to modern computing.

CPUs: The Versatile Taskmasters

CPUs serve as computers' central control units designed to handle various tasks with precision and reliability. They operate sequentially, executing one instruction at a time, and excel in tasks that demand high single-thread performance. This versatility allows CPUs to manage everything from basic word processing to complex simulations.

Key characteristics of CPUs include:

Low-latency performance: CPUs are optimised for tasks requiring quick decision-making and responsiveness.

Limited parallelism: Modern CPUs offer multiple cores, but their architecture prioritises serial processing.

Generality: CPUs are built for a wide array of applications, ensuring flexibility but often at the cost of specialised efficiency.

GPUs: Masters of Parallel Processing

Initially designed to accelerate rendering for graphics-intensive applications, GPUs have transformed into computational powerhouses. Their architecture is tailored for parallelism, enabling them to handle thousands of simultaneous tasks and making them indispensable for workloads like machine learning, simulations, and data analysis.

The defining characteristics of GPUs include:

High throughput: GPUs possess hundreds or thousands of cores, each capable of executing instructions concurrently.

Specialized focus: Their design is optimized for repetitive, data-parallel tasks, and they excel in matrix operations and vector calculations.

Enhanced scalability: GPUs can handle increasingly complex problems by leveraging their parallel architecture.

By complementing each other, CPUs and GPUs have redefined modern computing. CPUs oversee system-wide coordination while GPUs tackle compute-intensive tasks with unprecedented efficiency. This synergy is particularly evident in the gaming, artificial intelligence, and data analytics industries.

Parallel Processing Capabilities of GPUs

One of GPU's defining features is its unparalleled ability to perform parallel processing. Unlike CPUs, which prioritise low-latency, single-thread performance, GPUs are engineered to divide tasks into smaller components and execute them concurrently across multiple cores. This ability is transformative for tasks requiring massive computational power, such as training machine learning models, processing large datasets, and simulating physical phenomena.

The Role of CUDA Architecture

NVIDIA's CUDA (Compute Unified Device Architecture) has been instrumental in harnessing the power of parallel processing. CUDA allows developers to program GPUs directly, unlocking their potential for scientific computing, deep learning, and complex simulations. By providing tools and libraries, CUDA simplifies the process of optimising applications to use thousands of GPU cores efficiently.

Applications in AI and Machine Learning

Parallel processing has revolutionised artificial intelligence and machine learning by significantly reducing the time required to train and deploy models. Tasks such as image recognition, natural language processing, and generative AI rely on GPUs to process vast amounts of data in parallel. For example, training a neural network that might take weeks on a CPU can often be completed in hours with the right GPU setup.

Real-time Rendering and Simulations

The entertainment industry benefits immensely from GPU parallelism. Due to the concurrent execution of pixel, vertex, and geometry shaders, real-time rendering of complex 3D graphics in video games and movies is possible. Similarly, GPUs drive high-fidelity simulations for physics-based modeling, enabling realistic depictions of environments and interactions.

Advancements in Semiconductor Chip Capacity

The relentless pursuit of Moore's Law has propelled advancements in semiconductor technology, directly impacting GPUs. Each successive generation of GPU chips incorporates more transistors, improving performance and efficiency.

Shrinking Node Sizes

Modern GPUs are fabricated using advanced lithography techniques, with node sizes shrinking to as small as 3nm. This reduction allows for higher transistor density, reduced power consumption, and improved performance. These advancements have fueled the creation of GPUs capable of supporting real-time ray tracing, high-resolution gaming, and intensive AI computations.

Innovations in Memory Technology

High-bandwidth memory (HBM) and GDDR (Graphics Double Data Rate) memory technologies have become staples of modern GPUs. These innovations ensure rapid data transfer between the GPU and its memory, which is critical for applications requiring high throughput, such as 4K video rendering and neural network training.

Energy Efficiency and Sustainability

With increased capacity comes the challenge of energy efficiency. GPU manufacturers have made significant strides in reducing power consumption without compromising performance. Dynamic voltage and frequency scaling (DVFS) and advanced cooling solutions are among the strategies employed to address this challenge.

Key Products and Applications

NVIDIA has consistently led the GPU industry with groundbreaking products and technologies. Each product line caters to specific market needs, from gaming enthusiasts to AI researchers and data center operators.

GeForce GTX and RTX Series

The GeForce GTX and RTX series are NVIDIA's flagship gaming and professional applications offerings. The RTX series, in particular, introduced real-time ray tracing and DLSS (Deep Learning Super Sampling), redefining graphical fidelity and performance.

Applications:

- **Gaming:** High-resolution, immersive experiences for AAA titles.

- **Professional Content Creation:** Support for 3D modeling, video editing, and animation.

- **Virtual Reality:** Powering VR headsets with low-latency, high-quality graphics.

A and H Series, DGX Systems

NVIDIA's A and H series GPUs are designed for AI and data center applications. Combined with DGX systems, these GPUs provide unparalleled deep learning and high-performance computing (HPC) performance.

Applications:

- **AI Research:** Accelerating the training and inference of large-scale models.

- **Data Centers:** Supporting cloud-based AI workloads and high-speed analytics.

- **HPC:** Enabling simulations in genomics, weather forecasting, and quantum physics.

Tegra Series

The Tegra series is designed for small devices, balancing performance with energy efficiency. These chips are prevalent in automotive infotainment systems, smartphones, and IoT devices.

Applications:

- **Autonomous Vehicles:** Driving AI-powered decision-making systems.
- **Smart Devices:** Enhancing user experiences in mobile and embedded platforms.
- **Gaming Consoles:** Powering portable consoles like the Nintendo Switch.

Mellanox ConnectX SmartNICs and Quantum InfiniBand

NVIDIA's acquisition of Mellanox introduced networking solutions that complement GPU performance. ConnectX SmartNICs and Quantum InfiniBand ensure efficient data transfer, which is crucial for cloud computing and machine learning.

Applications:

- **Cloud Computing:** Facilitating high-speed data exchanges in multi-tenant environments.

- **AI Workloads:** Minimizing latency in distributed training setups.

- **Supercomputing:** Supporting petaflop-scale calculations in research institutions.

CUDA, AI Enterprise, and Drive

NVIDIA's software ecosystem, including CUDA, AI Enterprise, and Drive, empowers developers to unlock GPUs' full potential.

Applications:

- **CUDA:** CUDA enables researchers and engineers to develop GPU-accelerated applications.

- **AI Enterprise:** Streamlining the deployment of AI in enterprise environments.

- **Drive:** Powering autonomous vehicle platforms with real-time decision-making capabilities.

GPUs' operational characteristics, along with advancements in semiconductor technology and NVIDIA's innovative product lineup, underscore their transformative impact on computing. GPUs have become the backbone of modern technology, from powering gaming experiences and AI breakthroughs to enabling autonomous vehicles and cloud infrastructures. As the industry evolves, the synergy between GPUs, CPUs, and specialised tools will drive unprecedented advancements across domains.

CHAPTER 2

EARLY HISTORY (1990S)

The 1990s were a transformative decade for the technology industry, particularly for companies that dared to venture into the uncharted territories of graphics processing and gaming. Among the pioneers of this era was NVIDIA, a company that would later redefine the computing landscape. Founded in 1993, NVIDIA's story begins with a bold vision, a trio of visionary founders, and groundbreaking innovations that laid the foundation for its success.

Founding of NVIDIA in 1993

NVIDIA was officially established in April 1993 in Santa Clara, California, by Jensen Huang, Chris Malachowsky, and Curtis Priem. Each founder brought unique expertise to the venture. Jensen Huang, who became the company's first CEO, had a background in electrical engineering and computer science and experience at industry giants like LSI Logic and AMD. Chris Malachowsky, a seasoned engineer, contributed his deep technical acumen, while Curtis Priem, credited with designing the first graphics processor at Sun Microsystems, brought critical industry insights.

Their shared vision was ambitious: to build a company to revolutionise visual computing. At a time when personal computing was in its infancy, the trio foresaw the growing importance of high-performance graphics. They believed that 3D graphics technology would be pivotal in industries beyond gaming, including scientific research, entertainment, and virtual reality. Their mission was encapsulated in the company's mantra: "The world will be visual."

NVIDIA's journey began with an initial investment of $20 million from venture capital firms, an impressive feat for a fledgling startup in the highly competitive tech sector. This funding allowed the company to assemble a team of talented engineers and researchers. From the outset, NVIDIA focused on developing cutting-edge graphics processing units (GPUs) that could deliver unparalleled performance and realism.

The 1990s were characterised by rapid advancements in PC gaming, which provided an ideal testing ground for NVIDIA's technology. Recognising the immense potential of this market, the company concentrated on designing GPUs that catered to gamers' demanding requirements. Early on, NVIDIA embraced a strategy of innovation through rapid iteration, ensuring that its products stayed ahead of competitors.

Key Breakthroughs in the 1990s

NVIDIA's relentless pursuit of innovation led to several key breakthroughs during its early years. 1995, the company launched its first product, the NV1, a multimedia accelerator card. While the NV1 received mixed reviews due to its unconventional design, it demonstrated NVIDIA's commitment to pushing technological boundaries. The lessons learned from the NV1 informed the development of future products.

One of NVIDIA's significant milestones was introducing the RIVA 128 in 1997. The RIVA 128 was among the first GPUs to offer hardware acceleration for 3D graphics, setting a new standard for performance and visual fidelity. Its success marked NVIDIA's emergence as a major player in the graphics industry.

Launch of RIVA Series and RIVA TNT Processors

Building on the success of the RIVA 128, NVIDIA unveiled the RIVA TNT in 1998. The RIVA TNT (Twins-Texture) represented a leap forward in graphics technology. It introduced support for multi-texturing, allowing developers to layer multiple textures on 3D objects, resulting in more realistic visuals. The RIVA TNT's ability to process two textures simultaneously made it a favorite among gamers and developers.

The RIVA TNT was followed by the RIVA TNT2 in 1999, further enhancing performance and image quality. It offered higher clock speeds, improved color precision, and support for higher resolutions. These advancements solidified NVIDIA's reputation as a leader in the GPU market.

GeForce 256 and Partnership with Microsoft Xbox

NVIDIA's defining moment of the 1990s came with the launch of the GeForce 256 in 1999. Hailed as the world's first GPU, the GeForce 256 introduced hardware transformation and lighting (T&L), a revolutionary technology that offloaded complex calculations from the CPU to the GPU. This innovation enhanced gaming performance and opened new possibilities for developers, enabling them to create more complex and immersive 3D environments.

The GeForce 256's impact extended beyond gaming. Its capabilities attracted Microsoft's attention, leading to a groundbreaking partnership. In 1999, NVIDIA was selected as the GPU provider for Microsoft's upcoming Xbox gaming console. This collaboration marked a significant milestone for NVIDIA, positioning the company at the forefront of the console gaming industry.

Challenges and Triumphs

While remarkable achievements marked NVIDIA's journey in the 1990s, it was not without challenges. The company faced fierce competition from established players like 3dfx Interactive, ATI Technologies, and Matrox. To stay ahead, NVIDIA adopted an aggressive strategy of innovation, regularly introducing new products that outperformed their predecessors.

Another key factor in NVIDIA's success was its ability to cultivate strong relationships with game developers. By providing robust support and tools, NVIDIA optimised its GPUs for the latest games. This developer-centric approach contributed to the widespread adoption of NVIDIA's technology.

By the decade's end, NVIDIA had become a dominant force in the graphics industry. The innovations of the 1990s laid the groundwork for the company's future growth and influence. The introduction of the GeForce 256 marked the beginning of NVIDIA's GeForce product line, which would become a cornerstone of the company's success.

NVIDIA's journey in the 1990s exemplifies the power of vision, innovation, and determination. From its humble beginnings in a small office in Silicon Valley to its emergence as a leader in graphics technology, NVIDIA's early history is a testament to the transformative potential of bold ideas and the relentless pursuit of excellence.

CHAPTER 3

GAMING EXPANSION AND DIVERSIFICATION (2000s)

The 2000s marked a transformative era for NVIDIA as it solidified its presence in the gaming industry and ventured into new domains. This period witnessed NVIDIA's role as a pivotal innovator in gaming consoles, its collaboration with major technology players, its diversification into real-world applications, and its ability to navigate recognition and setbacks.

Role in Gaming Console Development

NVIDIA's commitment to pushing the boundaries of graphics technology found fertile ground in the gaming console industry. By the early 2000s, gaming had evolved into a primary entertainment medium, and NVIDIA seized the opportunity to shape the future of interactive entertainment. Its development of high-performance graphics processors catered to the growing demand for realistic visuals and immersive gameplay experiences.

One of NVIDIA's landmark achievements during this time was its collaboration with Microsoft for the original Xbox launched in

2001. The Xbox featured NVIDIA's custom-designed NV2A GPU, which set a new standard for console gaming by delivering superior graphics rendering and processing power. This partnership established NVIDIA as a crucial player in the console market and demonstrated its ability to adapt its technology to specific hardware requirements.

The company's involvement in console development did not stop with Microsoft. In 2006, NVIDIA played a key role in the release of Sony's PlayStation 3. Collaborating with Sony, NVIDIA provided the RSX "Reality Synthesizer" GPU, which worked in tandem with the PlayStation's cutting-edge Cell processor. The RSX chip enabled unprecedented graphical fidelity, supporting high-definition gaming and groundbreaking visual effects. NVIDIA's collaboration with these tech giants showcased its versatility and highlighted its position as a leader in the gaming industry.

Collaborations with Sony (PlayStation 3) and Microsoft (Xbox)

The partnerships with Sony and Microsoft were strategic business moves and technological milestones. The Xbox and PlayStation 3 collaborations demonstrated NVIDIA's capability to create specialised solutions tailored to the unique demands of console gaming. By working closely with Microsoft, NVIDIA delivered a

GPU that could handle the Xbox's ambitious goals of combining gaming, media playback, and online functionality. This collaboration laid the groundwork for Microsoft's success in entering the highly competitive console market.

Similarly, the PlayStation 3 partnership showcased NVIDIA's expertise in leveraging hardware to achieve cinematic visuals and dynamic gameplay. The RSX GPU was instrumental in powering some of the most visually stunning games of the era, including titles like Uncharted: Drake's Fortune and Metal Gear Solid 4: Guns of the Patriots. These collaborations underscored NVIDIA's role as a key enabler of immersive gaming experiences.

Diversification into Real-World Applications

While gaming remained a core focus, the 2000s also saw NVIDIA diversify its technology for real-world applications. The company recognised that the' power of GPUs extended far beyond gaming, paving the way for groundbreaking innovations in other industries.

One notable example was NVIDIA's collaboration with NASA on Mars simulations. NASA leveraged NVIDIA's GPUs to create detailed simulations of the Martian surface, enabling scientists to understand better the planet's terrain and plan rover missions with precision. This application of NVIDIA's technology demonstrated its potential to contribute to scientific discovery and exploration.

Another significant venture was NVIDIA's partnership with Audi, a leader in the automotive industry. Audi utilised NVIDIA's graphics chips to enhance the visual quality of vehicle interfaces and navigation systems. Integrating NVIDIA's GPUs into Audi's systems revolutionised how drivers interacted with their vehicles, setting a new standard for automotive technology. This collaboration highlighted NVIDIA's ability to adapt its expertise to diverse fields, expanding its influence beyond the gaming world.

Recognition and Setbacks

NVIDIA's achievements during the 2000s did not go unnoticed. In 2007, Forbes magazine named NVIDIA "Company of the Year," a testament to its innovation, growth, and impact on the technology sector. This recognition validated NVIDIA's efforts to push the boundaries of what was possible with GPUs and underscored its role as a trailblazer in the industry.

However, success was not without its challenges. NVIDIA faced significant setbacks during this period, including legal and manufacturing issues. A class-action lawsuit emerged due to defective graphics chips used in certain laptops. These defects, which caused overheating and system failures, tarnished NVIDIA's reputation and led to financial losses. The company's response involved a costly settlement and the implementation of measures to prevent similar issues in the future.

Additionally, NVIDIA faced a legal dispute with IBM over patent infringement claims. The settlement required NVIDIA to pay a substantial sum, highlighting the complexities of operating in a highly competitive and litigious industry. These challenges underscored the importance of adaptability and resilience in maintaining leadership in the technology sector.

The 2000s were a defining decade for NVIDIA, characterised by its expansion and diversification. The company's contributions to gaming consoles, collaborations with industry leaders like Sony and Microsoft, and ventures into real-world applications showcased its ability to innovate and adapt. Despite facing setbacks, NVIDIA's recognition as Forbes' "Company of the Year" in 2007 highlighted its enduring impact on the technology landscape. This era laid the foundation for NVIDIA's future endeavors, cementing its status as a graphics technology leader.

CHAPTER 4

THE RISE OF PARALLEL COMPUTING AND AI (2010s)

The 2010s marked a transformative period in computing history, characterised by the meteoric rise of parallel computing and artificial intelligence (AI). This era reshaped the technological landscape, revolutionising industries and redefining research, commerce, and daily life possibilities. Central to this revolution were advancements in hardware and software that enabled unprecedented computational efficiency and power.

Development of Parallel Computing

Parallel computing—the practice of performing multiple calculations simultaneously—emerged as a solution to the limitations of traditional, sequential processing. The ever-increasing demand for computational speed and power necessitated a shift in approach. By leveraging the capabilities of parallel processors, complex tasks could be divided into smaller sub-tasks, executed concurrently, and then recombined to yield faster and more efficient results.

Graphics Processing Units (GPUs), traditionally used to render visuals in video games and graphic-intensive applications, became pivotal in this shift. Due to their highly parallel structure, GPUs excelled at handling massive parallel tasks. By harnessing thousands of cores, GPUs could process vast amounts of data simultaneously, outperforming central processing units (CPUs) for specific workloads. This advancement paved the way for breakthroughs in scientific research, data analytics, and artificial intelligence.

Introduction of CUDA in 2006

A significant milestone in the evolution of parallel computing was NVIDIA's introduction of Compute Unified Device Architecture (CUDA) in 2006. CUDA was a groundbreaking parallel computing platform and programming model that enabled developers to harness the power of GPUs for general-purpose computing. Unlike traditional GPU programming, which required specialised knowledge, CUDA provided a more accessible and flexible environment, enabling a wider audience of developers to innovate.

CUDA's architecture allowed developers to write code in familiar programming languages like C, C++, and Fortran. This democratisation of GPU programming spurred the creation of many applications, particularly in areas that demanded high computational performance, such as image processing, scientific simulations, and AI model training. Although introduced before the 2010s, CUDA's impact flourished in this decade, becoming a cornerstone of modern AI and deep learning advancements.

Impact on AI and Deep Learning Applications

The convergence of parallel computing and AI created a seismic shift in the technological landscape. Deep learning, a subset of machine learning that mimics the human brain's neural networks, experienced a renaissance due to the computational power of GPUs. Thanks to GPUs' parallel processing capabilities, complex neural networks that previously required weeks or months to train could now be trained in a fraction of the time.

Notable achievements in AI during the 2010s included advancements in natural language processing, image recognition, and autonomous systems. GPUs were instrumental in training models such as AlexNet, ResNet, and GPT (Generative Pre-trained Transformer). These models set new benchmarks in their respective domains, showcasing the immense potential of combining parallel computing with AI methodologies.

Industries quickly adopted these advancements, integrating AI-driven solutions into healthcare, finance, automotive, and retail.

For example, GPUs enabled real-time medical image analysis, predictive financial modeling, and personalized shopping experiences. Parallel computing's scalability and efficiency also underpinned the development of autonomous vehicles, allowing systems to process sensor data in real time to navigate complex environments.

Strategic Acquisitions

To solidify its position as a leader in computing, NVIDIA pursued strategic acquisitions throughout the 2010s. These acquisitions aimed to bolster the company's technological capabilities, expand its market reach, and secure its dominance in emerging fields. Among the notable purchases were:

3Dfx Interactive: Though acquired earlier in 2000, the legacy of 3Dfx Interactive continued to influence NVIDIA's advancements in the 2010s. 3Dfx's expertise in graphics technology provided a foundation for NVIDIA's dominance in GPU development, enabling the company to stay ahead of competitors in gaming and professional visualisation markets.

PGI (Portland Group Inc.): Acquired in 2013, PGI was renowned for its high-performance compilers and development tools. This acquisition allowed NVIDIA to enhance its software ecosystem, providing developers with robust tools for optimising GPU-accelerated applications. PGI's technologies became integral to the success of CUDA, ensuring seamless integration and performance gains across diverse applications.

Icera: NVIDIA's acquisition of Icera in 2011 marked its entry into the mobile communications sector. Icera specialised in baseband processors, which are essential for mobile device connectivity. While NVIDIA eventually exited the mobile chip market, Icera's technology played a role in developing early Tegra products, setting the stage for innovations in automotive and embedded systems.

Mobile Computing and Automotive Innovations

Recognising the growing importance of mobile and automotive markets, NVIDIA made significant strides in these sectors during the 2010s. The launch of the Tegra processor series exemplified the company's commitment to pushing boundaries in mobile computing and embedded systems.

Launch of Tegra: Tegra is a line of system-on-chip (SoC) processors designed to deliver high performance while maintaining energy efficiency. The Tegra series found applications in various devices, from smartphones and tablets to gaming consoles like the NVIDIA Shield. These processors also became the backbone of

NVIDIA's automotive computing platform, DRIVE, which powers advanced driver-assistance systems (ADAS) and autonomous vehicles.

Partnerships with Toyota and Baidu: NVIDIA's foray into the automotive sector gained momentum through strategic partnerships with industry leaders such as Toyota and Baidu. Collaborations with Toyota focused on integrating NVIDIA's AI-powered DRIVE platform into next-generation vehicles, enabling features such as real-time object recognition, lane detection, and driver monitoring.

Similarly, NVIDIA's partnership with Baidu advanced the development of autonomous driving technologies in China. Baidu leveraged NVIDIA's GPUs and AI expertise to enhance its Apollo autonomous driving platform, achieving significant vehicle perception, mapping, and decision-making milestones.

The Broader Implications of Parallel Computing and AI

The developments of the 2010s extended far beyond technological advancements. They laid the groundwork for a new era of innovation, where the interplay between hardware and software created opportunities previously thought impossible. Parallel computing and AI drove progress in scientific research, leading to breakthroughs in genomics, climate modeling, and astrophysics. They also democratised technology, making powerful tools accessible to startups, researchers, and hobbyists alike.

Moreover, the rise of parallel computing and AI prompted discussions about ethics, privacy, and the societal impact of technology. As algorithms became more pervasive, concerns about bias, transparency, and data security emerged. These challenges underscored the need for responsible innovation, ensuring that the benefits of these technologies were equitably distributed.

The 2010s will be remembered as a decade of transformation, where parallel computing and AI emerged as catalysts for progress. NVIDIA played a pivotal role in shaping this era through innovations like CUDA, strategic acquisitions, and advancements in mobile and automotive computing. The convergence of parallel processing and AI redefined industries and inspired a new wave of creativity and exploration, setting the stage for the technological revolutions to come.

CHAPTER 5

THE AI RENAISSANCE AND MODERN CHALLENGES (2020s)

The 2020s ushered in a transformative era in artificial intelligence (AI), redefining industries and societies globally. At the heart of this revolution stood NVIDIA, a company whose technological innovations shaped the AI landscape. The decade witnessed groundbreaking advancements in AI capabilities, mainly through the interplay of deep learning algorithms and graphical processing unit (GPU) technologies. Yet, with progress came challenges, as NVIDIA navigated regulatory scrutiny, competitive pressures, and the complexities of global markets.

AI Breakthroughs and GPU Advancements

The 2020s marked an unprecedented surge in AI applications. Breakthroughs in natural language processing (NLP), generative AI, and autonomous systems have redefined the boundaries of machine capabilities. Central to these developments was NVIDIA's leadership in GPU technology. Originally designed for rendering complex graphics in video games, GPUs evolved into indispensable tools for AI training and inference due to their ability to process vast amounts of data in parallel.

NVIDIA's Ampere architecture, introduced in 2020, exemplified this trend. The Ampere GPUs offered unmatched performance for AI workloads, accelerating tasks ranging from image recognition to molecular simulations. Researchers and developers embraced these GPUs as they tackled increasingly complex problems in fields like healthcare, robotics, and climate science. For instance, AI models trained on NVIDIA GPUs facilitated breakthroughs in drug discovery, including the rapid development of COVID-19 vaccines.

As AI models grew more extensive and sophisticated, so did the demand for computational power. NVIDIA's A100 Tensor Core GPUs became a cornerstone for data centers worldwide, enabling companies to deploy AI solutions at scale. Combining tensor cores and cutting-edge software frameworks, such as NVIDIA's CUDA, provided unparalleled efficiency for training deep neural networks. These innovations positioned NVIDIA as the go-to partner for enterprises seeking to harness AI's transformative potential.

Omniverse Platform for 3D Imaging and Design

Another milestone in NVIDIA's journey was the launch of the Omniverse platform, a revolutionary collaborative 3D design and simulation tool. Announced in 2021, the Omniverse allowed creators, engineers, and scientists to work together in a shared virtual environment. Leveraging NVIDIA's GPUs and AI capabilities, the platform enabled real-time collaboration on projects ranging from architectural designs to virtual film sets.

The Omniverse's significance extends beyond its technical features. By bridging the gap between industries, it became a linchpin for the emerging metaverse—a shared digital space where people interact, work, and play. Companies in entertainment, manufacturing, and retail adopted the Omniverse to simulate real-world scenarios, optimize processes, and create immersive experiences. For example, automotive manufacturers used the platform to design and test virtual prototypes, reducing time to market and costs.

NVIDIA's vision for the Omniverse underscored the company's broader mission: to enable innovation through powerful tools that empower creators. As the metaverse gained traction, the Omniverse solidified NVIDIA's reputation as a leader in shaping the future of virtual and augmented realities.

Impact of ChatGPT and AI-Driven Demand for NVIDIA Chips

The release of OpenAI's ChatGPT in late 2022 marked a watershed moment in AI's evolution. This generative AI model demonstrated unprecedented capabilities in understanding and generating human-like text, sparking widespread interest and adoption. Behind the scenes,

NVIDIA's GPUs played a critical role in powering ChatGPT's training and deployment.

ChatGPT's success catalyzed a surge in demand for AI infrastructure. Enterprises across sectors sought to integrate similar AI solutions into their operations, driving exponential growth in the need for high-performance GPUs. NVIDIA capitalized on this trend by expanding its product offerings and forging partnerships with cloud service providers, such as Amazon Web Services (AWS) and Microsoft Azure. These collaborations ensured businesses could access NVIDIA's cutting-edge hardware and software for their AI initiatives.

The ripple effects of ChatGPT extended to NVIDIA's bottom line. The company experienced record-breaking revenue growth as demand for its AI-focused GPUs skyrocketed. This success underscored the symbiotic relationship between AI advancements and the underlying hardware that makes them possible. NVIDIA's ability to anticipate and meet this demand solidified its position as a linchpin in the AI ecosystem.

Regulatory Scrutiny and Antitrust Challenges

Despite its achievements, NVIDIA faced mounting regulatory scrutiny in the 2020s. As the company's influence grew, so did concerns about its market dominance and competitive practices. Regulators in the United States, Europe, and China launched investigations into NVIDIA's business operations, examining pricing strategies, market concentration, and potential anti-competitive behavior.

One focal point of regulatory scrutiny was NVIDIA's role in the AI and semiconductor markets. Critics argued that the company's dominance in GPUs gave it undue leverage over competitors and customers. For instance, NVIDIA's acquisition of Mellanox Technologies in 2020 raised eyebrows due to its potential impact on the networking and data center markets. While the deal ultimately received regulatory approval, it highlighted the challenges of navigating complex global antitrust frameworks.

Attempted Arm Ltd. Acquisition

NVIDIA's most controversial regulatory challenge came in 2020 with its attempted acquisition of Arm Ltd., a British semiconductor and software design company. Valued at $40 billion, the deal aimed to combine NVIDIA's GPU expertise with Arm's CPU architecture to create a powerhouse in AI and computing.

However, the proposed acquisition faced fierce opposition from regulators, competitors, and industry stakeholders. Critics argued that the deal would stifle competition, given Arm's pivotal role as a neutral supplier of chip designs to various companies. Concerns about intellectual property access and potential conflicts of interest dominated the discourse.

In 2022, NVIDIA abandoned the acquisition after prolonged investigations and regulatory hurdles. The failed deal highlighted the growing complexities of navigating global regulatory environments, particularly in the semiconductor industry. Despite the setback, NVIDIA's strategic vision remained intact as it pursued innovation through organic growth and partnerships.

Ongoing Investigations in the U.S., Europe, and China

NVIDIA's global footprint exposed it to diverse regulatory landscapes, each with its challenges and priorities. In the United States, the Federal Trade Commission (FTC) intensified its scrutiny of tech giants, including NVIDIA. Investigations focused on the company's pricing practices, competitive strategies, and potential consumer harm.

In Europe, the European Commission launched probes into NVIDIA's market behavior, particularly its role in the AI and cloud computing sectors. European regulators emphasised the need to maintain a level playing field and prevent market distortions. Similarly, Chinese authorities examined NVIDIA's operations, reflecting broader geopolitical tensions and concerns about technological dependencies.

Despite these challenges, NVIDIA remained committed to compliance and cooperation with regulators. The company's proactive approach, including transparency initiatives and stakeholder engagement, helped mitigate some of the risks associated with regulatory scrutiny. However, the investigations underscored the growing importance of ethical and responsible business practices in an era of heightened accountability.

CHAPTER 6

BLACKWELL INNOVATIONS AND THE FUTURE

Overview of Blackwell Architecture

Blackwell, NVIDIA's latest architectural breakthrough, represents a significant leap in computational capabilities. Named after David Blackwell, the esteemed statistician and mathematician, the architecture reflects the company's commitment to combining innovation with precision. Blackwell's design builds upon the strengths of its predecessor, Hopper, while introducing numerous advancements tailored for artificial intelligence (AI), high-performance computing (HPC), and data-intensive tasks.

The Blackwell architecture redefines performance efficiency at its core by integrating cutting-edge design philosophies. Its modular structure allows for scalable deployment across diverse workloads. Blackwell achieves unprecedented speed and efficiency by enhancing parallelism and optimising memory throughput. The architecture's focus on maximising computational density while minimising energy consumption positions it as a cornerstone for next-generation data centers and AI infrastructures.

Key Features

The Blackwell architecture introduces a suite of powerful chips that set new benchmarks in computational performance. These chips are engineered to handle the growing complexity of AI models, from generative AI applications to intricate simulations in scientific research. Central to this achievement is the inclusion of transformer engines, which are specifically optimised for large-scale machine learning tasks. These engines excel at accelerating training and inference for transformer-based models, enabling faster development cycles for AI applications.

A key differentiator in Blackwell's design is the advanced NVLink interconnect technology. NVLink, now in its latest iteration, provides a significant boost in bandwidth and connectivity between GPUs. This enhancement ensures seamless communication within multi-GPU setups, enabling applications to scale efficiently across multiple devices. The introduction of NVLink Switch further amplifies the architecture's capability to support large-scale, distributed computing environments.

The Blackwell chips also incorporate improvements in tensor core technology. These upgrades enhance mixed-precision computing, allowing developers to perform better without compromising accuracy. This feature particularly benefits AI workloads, where precision and speed are paramount.

GB200 Grace Blackwell Superchip and Its Applications

One of the standout innovations within the Blackwell lineup is the GB200 Grace Blackwell Superchip. This hybrid solution combines the power of NVIDIA's Grace CPU with the advanced capabilities of the Blackwell GPU. The integration of these two components creates a versatile platform that excels in diverse applications.

The GB200 addresses the growing demand for AI and HPC workloads. By leveraging the synergy between the Grace CPU's high memory bandwidth and the Blackwell GPU's computational prowess, the Superchip delivers exceptional performance in natural language processing, autonomous vehicle development, and molecular dynamics simulations. Its ease of handling data-intensive workloads makes it a preferred choice for enterprises aiming to accelerate their AI initiatives.

In addition to its performance advantages, the GB200 is also tailored for energy efficiency. Its design prioritises power optimisation, making it suitable for deployment in sustainable computing environments. Industries ranging from healthcare to finance are already exploring the potential of the GB200 to transform their operations, demonstrating its versatility and impact.

AI-Focused Product and Software Advancements

The Blackwell architecture is accompanied by a suite of AI-focused products and software advancements that enhance its capabilities.

NVIDIA has introduced a range of libraries and frameworks optimised for Blackwell, ensuring that developers can fully leverage its potential. Key offerings include improvements to the CUDA platform, which now supports advanced features unique to Blackwell's design.

One notable software innovation is the introduction of AI Workbench, a streamlined environment for developing, training, and deploying AI models. This tool integrates seamlessly with the Blackwell ecosystem, enabling researchers and engineers to experiment with complex models without encountering bottlenecks. Additionally, Blackwell's support for NVIDIA Triton Inference Server ensures the efficient deployment of AI models across various hardware configurations.

Another highlight is the focus on AI democratisation. NVIDIA aims to empower a broader audience to engage with AI technologies by providing tools that simplify the development process. This approach aligns with the company's vision of making AI accessible to all, fostering innovation across industries.

DGX Cloud Platform and Partnerships with Cloud Service Providers

The DGX Cloud platform is pivotal to NVIDIA's strategy to extend Blackwell's reach. DGX Cloud enables organisations to access Blackwell's capabilities without investing in on-premises infrastructure by offering a cloud-based solution. This approach democratises access to high-performance computing, making it feasible for startups and smaller enterprises to leverage state-of-the-art technology.

Partnerships with leading cloud service providers, including AWS, Microsoft Azure, and Google Cloud, have been instrumental in expanding the adoption of DGX Cloud. These collaborations ensure that customers can integrate NVIDIA's solutions into their existing workflows with minimal friction. By offering flexible subscription models, DGX Cloud provides organisations the scalability and agility to respond to evolving business demands.

The impact of DGX Cloud is evident in its adoption across diverse sectors. From accelerating drug discovery in the pharmaceutical industry to enhancing recommendation systems in e-commerce, the platform has demonstrated its ability to drive innovation. Its integration with Blackwell ensures that users benefit from the latest advancements in AI and HPC, further solidifying its position as a game-changer in the cloud computing landscape.

Collaborations with Software Makers

NVIDIA's collaboration with software makers such as Ansys, Cadence, and Synopsys underscores its commitment to creating a comprehensive ecosystem around the Blackwell architecture. These partnerships aim to optimise industry-specific applications, enabling users to harness the full potential of NVIDIA's technology.

Ansys, a leader in engineering simulation, has integrated Blackwell's capabilities into its software suite to accelerate computational fluid dynamics and structural analysis. By leveraging the architecture's advanced computational power, Ansys users can achieve faster simulation times and more accurate results, driving innovation in aerospace and automotive engineering.

Cadence, known for its electronic design automation (EDA) tools, has similarly benefited from the Blackwell architecture. The collaboration has enhanced chip design and verification tasks performance, enabling engineers to streamline their workflows. Blackwell's ability to efficiently handle large-scale computations has proven invaluable in addressing the complexities of modern semiconductor design.

Synopsys, another key player in the EDA industry, has leveraged Blackwell's capabilities to accelerate software development for AI hardware. By optimising tools for the architecture, Synopsys has facilitated the creation of more efficient and robust AI systems, furthering advancements in machine learning and data processing.

The Road Ahead: Blackwell's Role in Shaping the FutureAs industries continue to embrace AI and HPC, the Blackwell architecture stands poised to play a central role in shaping the future of technology. Its innovative design and ecosystem of supporting tools and partnerships position it as a transformative force across sectors. From enabling breakthroughs in scientific research to powering intelligent applications,

Blackwell exemplifies NVIDIA's vision of accelerating the world's transition to AI-driven solutions.

NVIDIA's commitment to sustainability and inclusivity will drive further advancements in the Blackwell ecosystem. By addressing the challenges of energy efficiency and accessibility, the company aims to create a more equitable and sustainable technological landscape. With its unparalleled capabilities and forward-thinking design, the Blackwell architecture represents a significant step toward realising this vision.

CHAPTER 7

THE NVIDIA GEFORCE RTX 50-SERIES

The Nvidia GeForce RTX 50 series represents the cutting edge of graphics technology, setting new benchmarks in gaming and professional graphics performance. Designed with the Blackwell architecture at its core, the RTX 50 series not only builds upon the strengths of its predecessors but also introduces groundbreaking features that redefine expectations in the GPU market.

Features of the RTX 50-Series

The RTX 50-series is a culmination of Nvidia's years of innovation in GPU technology. Key features include:

Blackwell Architecture: A leap forward from the Ada Lovelace architecture, the Blackwell architecture enhances computational efficiency and introduces new technologies that improve real-time ray tracing, AI-driven workloads, and general performance.

Improved Tensor and RT Cores: The RTX 50-series boasts fourth-generation Tensor Cores and third-generation RT Cores, offering significant advancements in AI processing and ray tracing capabilities.

Enhanced DLSS Technology: The series introduces DLSS 4.0, which leverages advanced AI models to deliver superior frame rates and image quality, making 8K gaming a reality.

Energy Efficiency: With a focus on sustainability, the RTX 50-series features improved energy efficiency, reducing power consumption while maintaining high performance.

Massive VRAM Capacities: With memory configurations reaching up to 24GB for the flagship model, the RTX 50-series supports demanding applications like 3D rendering, AI development, and high-resolution gaming.

PCIe Gen 5.0 Support: Offering increased bandwidth, the RTX 50-series ensures compatibility with the latest motherboards, enabling faster data transfer rates and reduced bottlenecks.

Blackwell Architecture Upgrades

The Blackwell architecture is a monumental upgrade, refining and expanding upon the foundation set by the Ada Lovelace architecture. Two of the most significant advancements are in the Tensor Cores and RT Cores:

Tensor Cores: The fourth-generation Tensor Cores in the RTX 50-series bring unprecedented AI acceleration. This enhanced computational power benefits from tasks like AI-based upscaling, real-time content generation, and deep learning models. The new cores also support mixed-precision calculations, offering improved performance for AI workloads without compromising accuracy.

RT Cores: Ray tracing has become a hallmark of Nvidia GPUs, and the third-generation RT Cores take this to new heights. They offer better hardware-accelerated ray-triangle intersection rates, leading to more realistic lighting, reflections, and shadows. These cores also introduce dynamic denoising features, which enhance visual fidelity in real-time applications.

Together, these upgrades enable the RTX 50 series to deliver stunning visuals and unmatched performance in gaming, content creation, and professional workloads.

Detailed Specifications

The RTX 50-series includes a range of GPUs catering to different performance needs. Below is a breakdown of the specifications for the primary models in the lineup:

RTX 5090

CUDA Cores: 20,000

Base/Boost Clock Speeds: 2.5 GHz / 3.2 GHz

VRAM: 24GB GDDR7

Memory Bandwidth: 1.2 TB/s

Power Consumption: 450W

Performance Highlights: The RTX 5090 is the flagship model, delivering exceptional performance for 8K gaming and professional rendering tasks.

RTX 5080

CUDA Cores: 17,000

Base/Boost Clock Speeds: 2.3 GHz / 3.0 GHz

VRAM: 20GB GDDR7

Memory Bandwidth: 1.0 TB/s

Power Consumption: 375W

Performance Highlights: Positioned as a high-end GPU, the RTX 5080 balances power and efficiency, making it ideal for 4K gaming and content creation.

RTX 5070 Ti

CUDA Cores: 14,500

Base/Boost Clock Speeds: 2.2 GHz / 2.8 GHz

VRAM: 16GB GDDR7

Memory Bandwidth: 800 GB/s

Power Consumption: 300W

Performance Highlights: With excellent performance for 1440p gaming, the RTX 5070 Ti is a mid-range powerhouse.

RTX 5070

CUDA Cores: 12,000

Base/Boost Clock Speeds: 2.1 GHz / 2.6 GHz

VRAM: 12GB GDDR7

Memory Bandwidth: 700 GB/s

Power Consumption: 250W

Performance Highlights: The RTX 5070 is a more affordable entry point to the RTX 50 series, perfect for gamers and casual creators.

Comparison with Previous Generations

The RTX 50-series builds upon the advancements introduced in the RTX 40-series (Ada Lovelace) and RTX 30-series (Ampere), delivering significant improvements in various areas:

Performance

Thanks to its enhanced architecture and higher core counts, the RTX 50 series provides up to 2x the performance of the RTX 40 series in specific workloads.

Real-time ray tracing is significantly faster, with new algorithms reducing rendering times.

Memory

GDDR7 memory in the RTX 50-series improves data transfer rates, enabling smoother performance in high-resolution gaming and professional applications.

Memory capacities are larger across the lineup, supporting more complex workflows and future-proofing the GPUs.

Energy Efficiency

The Blackwell architecture introduces power-saving features, reducing overall energy consumption compared to the RTX 40-series while maintaining higher performance levels.

Improved thermal management ensures that GPUs operate at optimal temperatures, even under heavy loads.

AI Capabilities

DLSS 4.0 in the RTX 50-series surpasses the capabilities of DLSS 3.0, offering better frame generation and image reconstruction.

Enhanced Tensor Cores enable faster AI-driven processes like content creation and machine learning.

Advancements in Performance, Memory, and Energy Efficiency

The RTX 50-series introduces several advancements that set it apart from its predecessors:

Performance

Higher CUDA core counts and improved clock speeds ensure that the RTX 50 series excels in gaming and professional tasks.

The GPUs are optimized for DirectX 12 Ultimate and Vulkan, providing unparalleled performance in modern games.

Memory

The transition to GDDR7 memory significantly boosts bandwidth and reduces latency, enabling smoother performance in demanding scenarios.

Larger VRAM capacities ensure the RTX 50-series can handle the most memory-intensive applications, such as 8K video editing and large-scale simulations.

Energy Efficiency

Nvidia's focus on sustainability is evident in the RTX 50-series, which offers better performance per watt than any previous generation.

Advanced power management features dynamically adjust GPU performance based on workload, minimizing energy usage without sacrificing speed.

The Nvidia GeForce RTX 50 series is evidence of the relentless pace of innovation in GPU technology. By combining the revolutionary Blackwell architecture with advancements in performance, memory, and energy efficiency, Nvidia has once again redefined the possibilities of gaming and professional graphics. The RTX 50 series delivers on every front, setting a new standard for what GPUs can achieve.

CHAPTER 8

NVIDIA'S IMPACT ON EMERGING TECHNOLOGIES

The pace of technological innovation in the 21st century has been unprecedented, and NVIDIA stands at the heart of this transformation. Once a company known primarily for its gaming GPUs, NVIDIA has evolved into a global leader driving advancements across artificial intelligence (AI), the metaverse, generative AI models, and various industries, such as healthcare, finance, and automotive. This chapter explores NVIDIA's role in shaping these emerging technologies and considers the potential future directions of its groundbreaking innovations.

Pioneering Artificial Intelligence (AI)

NVIDIA's contributions to artificial intelligence have been revolutionary. The company's GPUs have become the gold standard for AI research and development, thanks to their ability to efficiently process massive amounts of data. With the introduction of CUDA in 2006, NVIDIA laid the groundwork for

GPU-accelerated computing, enabling researchers to train AI models faster and more effectively than ever before.

NVIDIA's Tensor Core GPUs have transformed neural network training and inference in AI. Tensor Cores, specialized units for AI workloads, optimize matrix multiplication and other computationally intensive tasks critical for deep learning applications. These innovations have catalyzed natural language processing (NLP), computer vision, and speech recognition breakthroughs. Technologies like OpenAI's GPT models and DeepMind's AlphaFold rely heavily on NVIDIA's hardware and software ecosystem, underscoring the company's pivotal role in advancing AI research.

Moreover, NVIDIA's AI platforms, such as NVIDIA DGX systems, have become integral to enterprises aiming to integrate AI into their operations. From autonomous vehicles to recommendation engines, NVIDIA's GPUs power solutions that redefine industries, demonstrating the company's unparalleled influence on the AI landscape.

Enabling the Metaverse

The concept of the metaverse—a virtual world where individuals can interact, work, and play—has captured the imagination of technologists and creatives alike. NVIDIA has positioned itself as a critical enabler of the metaverse through its Omniverse platform, a groundbreaking suite of tools for creating and simulating virtual environments.

NVIDIA Omniverse leverages the company's powerful GPUs and AI technologies to deliver real-time simulations and photorealistic graphics. This platform allows developers, designers, and engineers to collaborate seamlessly in shared virtual spaces, paving the way for innovation in the architecture, media, and entertainment industries. Omniverse's support for Universal Scene Description (USD), an open standard developed by Pixar, ensures compatibility across tools and applications, fostering a more interconnected metaverse ecosystem.

Beyond its technical capabilities, NVIDIA's Omniverse is driving sustainability in industries such as manufacturing. By enabling digital twin-virtual replicas of physical assets, companies can optimize operations, reduce waste, and accelerate decision-making. The synergy between NVIDIA's hardware and software solutions is integral to the metaverse's growth, solidifying the company's role as a cornerstone of this emerging technology.

Transforming Generative AI Models

Generative AI models, capable of creating text, images, music, and more, represent a paradigm shift in artificial intelligence. NVIDIA's technology has been instrumental in the rise of these models, providing the computational power necessary to train them at scale.

One of NVIDIA's key contributions to generative AI is its collaboration with leading research institutions and companies. Models like DALL-E, Stable Diffusion, and ChatGPT rely on NVIDIA's GPUs to handle the immense computational demands of training and inference. NVIDIA's A100 and H100 GPUs, with their high memory bandwidth and multi-instance GPU capabilities, are optimized for these workloads, enabling faster development cycles and more sophisticated AI applications.

In addition to hardware, NVIDIA's software tools, such as NVIDIA Triton Inference Server and NVIDIA NeMo, empower developers to deploy generative AI models efficiently. Triton simplifies serving AI models in production environments, while NeMo provides a framework for building domain-specific applications, such as chatbots and virtual assistants. These tools make generative AI accessible to a broader audience, democratizing innovation and fostering creativity across industries.

Contributions to Key Industries

NVIDIA's impact extends far beyond AI and the metaverse. The company's technology is transforming healthcare, finance, and automotive industries, driving innovation and improving outcomes.

Healthcare

In healthcare, NVIDIA's GPUs are accelerating medical research and diagnosis. AI-powered medical imaging, drug discovery, and genomics tools rely on NVIDIA's hardware to analyze vast datasets with unparalleled speed and accuracy. For instance, NVIDIA Clara, a healthcare-specific AI platform, supports applications ranging from radiology to surgical simulations. NVIDIA is reshaping how healthcare is delivered by enabling faster diagnoses and personalized treatment plans.

Finance

NVIDIA's technology optimises high-frequency trading, risk management, and fraud detection in the financial sector. GPUs' ability to process massive volumes of data in real time makes them ideal for these applications. NVIDIA's AI frameworks also support natural language processing tasks, such as analyzing market sentiment and predicting trends, giving financial institutions a competitive edge.

Automotive

The automotive industry is undergoing a seismic shift toward electrification and autonomy, and NVIDIA is at the forefront of this transformation. The NVIDIA DRIVE platform provides a comprehensive solution for developing self-driving cars, combining AI, simulation, and high-performance computing. NVIDIA is shaping the future of transportation by enabling advanced driver-assistance systems (ADAS) and autonomous vehicle capabilities.

Future Directions for NVIDIA Technology

As NVIDIA continues pushing the boundaries of what's possible, several key trends will likely define its future trajectory. These include the expansion of AI capabilities, the evolution of quantum computing, and a growing focus on sustainability.

AI at the Edge

NVIDIA's investment in edge computing is set to revolutionize industries by bringing AI closer to where data is generated. From smart cities to industrial automation, edge AI applications powered by NVIDIA's Jetson platform will enable real-time decision-making with minimal latency.

Quantum Computing

Although still in its infancy, quantum computing holds the potential to solve problems beyond the reach of classical computers. NVIDIA's cuQuantum SDK, designed for accelerating quantum simulations, positions the company as a leader in this emerging field. By bridging the gap between quantum and classical computing, NVIDIA aims to unlock new scientific discovery and optimization possibilities.

Sustainability Initiatives

As climate change concerns grow, NVIDIA prioritizes sustainability in its operations and products. The company's energy-efficient GPUs and data center solutions are reducing carbon footprints while enabling breakthroughs in renewable energy research and climate modeling. NVIDIA's commitment to sustainability aligns with its broader mission to use technology for the greater good.

NVIDIA's impact on emerging technologies is profound and far-reaching. From powering AI breakthroughs to enabling the metaverse and transforming industries, the company has redefined the limits of innovation. As it continues to explore new frontiers, NVIDIA's technology will undoubtedly play a pivotal role in shaping the future, driving progress across AI, generative models, and beyond. The story of NVIDIA is not just one of technological achievement but of a vision to create a smarter, more connected, and sustainable world.

CONCLUSION

NVIDIA's journey from a fledgling graphics card manufacturer to a global leader in AI and GPU technology represents one of the most remarkable success stories in the tech industry. Founded in 1993, the company's innovative spirit and relentless pursuit of excellence have been instrumental in shaping the landscape of computing, gaming, artificial intelligence (AI), and data science. Throughout its evolution, NVIDIA has consistently pushed the boundaries of what GPUs can achieve, transitioning from their initial role in rendering graphics to becoming indispensable tools in solving some of the world's most complex computational challenges.

From its early days, NVIDIA demonstrated a clear vision and ambition. The release of the RIVA 128 in 1997 marked the company's first major milestone, establishing itself as a serious contender in the GPU market. However, it was the introduction of the GeForce 256 in 1999—touted as the world's first GPU—that solidified NVIDIA's position as a trailblazer. This innovation not only revolutionized gaming but also laid the groundwork for the company's future ventures into high-performance computing.

One of NVIDIA's most transformative moments came with the development of CUDA (Compute Unified Device Architecture) in 2006. By enabling developers to harness the parallel processing power of GPUs for general-purpose computing, CUDA became a game-changer, unlocking new possibilities in fields such as scientific research, medical imaging, and financial modeling. This was a pivotal step that propelled NVIDIA beyond gaming and into the broader realm of computational science.

In the 2010s, NVIDIA's focus shifted towards artificial intelligence, an area where GPUs proved uniquely suited for handling the massive parallel computations required for deep learning. The launch of the Tesla series GPUs and the subsequent introduction of the Volta architecture in 2017 underscored the company's commitment to AI. These advancements were crucial in accelerating natural language processing, autonomous vehicles, and robotics breakthroughs.

The Ampere architecture, unveiled in 2020, marked another leap forward. Designed to deliver unparalleled performance for AI and data analytics workloads, Ampere GPUs quickly became the backbone of cloud computing platforms and supercomputers worldwide. At the same time, NVIDIA expanded its ecosystem by acquiring Mellanox Technologies, further enhancing its capabilities in high-performance networking.

NVIDIA's achievements extend beyond hardware. The company's software solutions, such as TensorRT and cuDNN, have empowered developers to optimize AI applications, while platforms like Omniverse have redefined collaboration and simulation in 3D environments. These efforts have cemented NVIDIA's reputation as a holistic provider of cutting-edge technologies.

As NVIDIA looks to the future, it faces significant challenges and immense opportunities. The rapid pace of technological advancements demands continuous innovation, while global economic uncertainties and geopolitical tensions pose risks to supply chains and market stability. Despite these obstacles, NVIDIA remains well-positioned to lead the next wave of technological progress.

One of the most pressing challenges is the growing competition in the GPU market. Companies like AMD and Intel aggressively invest in GPU technologies, seeking to erode NVIDIA's market share. To maintain its leadership, NVIDIA must innovate at an unprecedented pace, delivering products that outperform competitors in performance, energy efficiency, and value.

The rise of custom silicon and specialized accelerators also presents a potential threat. As companies like Google, Apple, and Amazon develop their chips tailored for specific workloads, NVIDIA may face further pressure to differentiate its offerings. However, this trend also opens opportunities for collaboration and integration, particularly in AI and cloud computing.

Energy efficiency is another critical area of focus. As data centers consume increasing global electricity, there is mounting pressure to develop more sustainable technologies. NVIDIA's advancements in energy-efficient architectures, such as the Hopper series, demonstrate its commitment to addressing this issue. By prioritizing sustainability, NVIDIA can position itself as a leader in green computing, appealing to environmentally conscious customers and investors.

The ongoing evolution of AI presents unparalleled opportunities for NVIDIA. As industries embrace AI-driven solutions, the demand for powerful GPUs will continue to grow. NVIDIA's investment in AI-specific hardware, such as the DGX systems and Jetson platform, ensures it remains at the forefront of this transformation. Moreover, the company's collaborations with leading research institutions and enterprises position it as a key enabler of AI innovation.

Another emerging frontier, the metaverse, offers exciting possibilities for NVIDIA. With its Omniverse platform, the company is uniquely equipped to drive advancements in virtual reality (VR), augmented reality (AR), and digital twins. These technologies can potentially revolutionize industries ranging from entertainment and education to manufacturing and healthcare.

Quantum computing represents another long-term opportunity. While still in its infancy, quantum computing promises to solve problems currently intractable for classical computers. NVIDIA's expertise in GPUs and parallel processing could play a crucial role in bridging the gap between classical and quantum computing, paving the way for hybrid solutions that leverage the strengths of both paradigms.

NVIDIA's commitment to education and workforce development is also noteworthy. The company is fostering the next generation of AI and GPU developers by offering resources like the NVIDIA Deep Learning Institute and collaborating with universities worldwide. This approach strengthens NVIDIA's ecosystem and ensures a steady pipeline of talent to drive future innovations.

In the face of these opportunities, NVIDIA must navigate regulatory challenges and ethical considerations. As AI becomes more pervasive, data privacy, bias, and accountability issues will require careful attention. NVIDIA's proactive stance on ethical AI development and its collaboration with industry stakeholders will be critical in addressing these concerns.

Looking ahead, NVIDIA's vision extends beyond technological innovation. The company's commitment to corporate social responsibility, diversity, and inclusion reflects a broader understanding of its societal role. By fostering a culture of innovation and inclusivity, NVIDIA is shaping the future of technology and contributing to a more equitable and sustainable world.

NVIDIA's journey is a testament to the power of vision, innovation, and resilience. From pioneering the first GPU to leading the AI revolution, the company has consistently pushed the boundaries of what is possible. While challenges remain, NVIDIA's track record of adaptability and excellence positions it as a driving force in the tech industry.

As we conclude this exploration of NVIDIA's evolution, it is clear that the company's impact extends far beyond GPUs. By enabling breakthroughs in AI, scientific research, and digital experiences, NVIDIA has transformed how we live, work, and interact with technology. The road ahead is filled with uncertainty and promise, but one thing is sure: NVIDIA will continue to shape the future, one innovation at a time.

www.ingramcontent.com/pod-product-compliance
Lightning Source LLC
LaVergne TN
LVHW051606050326
832903LV00033B/4382